In the Tender Embrace of God's Mercy

Prayers, Meditations and Reflections
Celebrating the Year of Mercy

In memory of Fr Seamus Cullen

GARETH BYRNE

VERITAS

Published 2015 by Veritas Publications
7–8 Lower Abbey Street
Dublin 1, Ireland
publications@veritas.ie
www.veritas.ie

ISBN 978 1 84730 664 7

Designed by Heather Costello, Veritas Publications
Printed in the Republic of Ireland by Walsh Colour Print, Co. Kerry

Veritas books are printed on paper made from the wood pulp of
managed forests. For every tree felled, at least one tree is planted,
thereby renewing natural resources.

Introduction

Fifty years after the end of Vatican II, Pope Francis has invited us to reflect on the loving-kindness of the heart of our God. The Jubilee Year of Mercy is a celebration of God's goodness in our lives and a call to prayer and action. Pope Francis asks us, time and again, to rejoice with him in the all-embracing love of God. He reminds us of the words of Jesus: 'be merciful, just as your Father is merciful' (Luke 6: 36).

The motto for the Year of Mercy, 'Merciful like the Father', is an acknowledgement of God's merciful love in the life of the Christian and of our capacity to live likewise. For the Christian, the Word of God made flesh, Jesus Christ, embodies the mercy of God, bringing God's love into high relief in our world: 'Jesus Christ is the face of God's mercy' (*Misericordiae vultus*, 1). Jesus proclaimed the mercy of God, not only by his life-giving words and healing actions, but by his loving sacrifice for all God's people on the Cross. After two thousand years, the Holy Spirit still whispers to our world of the tender mercy of God, revealed to us definitively in Jesus Christ, our good shepherd and constant companion. Christ is available to us when we turn to him in prayer, when we meet him in our neighbour, when we gather as two or three in his name, when we celebrate his generous presence in the sacraments, when we love as he has loved us.

This book seeks to help us live in and feel God's mercy. Some of the prayers and reflections you will already know and love. Others will be new to you. You will find relevant passages from Scripture, from Vatican II and from *Share the Good News: National Directory for Catechesis in Ireland*. Some pages are designed to support time spent with Christ in the embrace of his Father's mercy. Others help us to pray into a response, reaching out to those on the margins, those lost perhaps, or searching for love. We are reminded that we, and they, are beautiful in God's eyes and loved beyond compare. We find ourselves blessed by God, who loves us with an everlasting love. Having experienced God's mercy we realise ourselves missioned to be merciful too.

'Blessed are the merciful for they will receive mercy.'
(Matthew 5:7)

This book provides a series of prompts for prayer and meditation. Take one page at a time, or perhaps just one phrase, and reflect on it in the presence of the Lord. Let Jesus speak to you. Enter into conversation with him for whatever time you may have. Stay with the text a while and make it your own. Allow Jesus to draw you to himself and allow yourself to experience the love of God. You can do this in a church. You can pray and reflect on the themes here, in a quiet place at home, sitting in your garden or on a bus, when you walk in the local park or by the sea. You can use this book as a focus for prayer or conversation with a group of parishioners or friends. Ask the Holy Spirit to encourage you to find a deep-felt response in your life.

If this book has been helpful, suggest it to those going through hard times or feeling dejected, those who sense themselves unforgiven or unforgiving, those suffering illness or anxiety, and those who have found hope and peace again. Listening quietly with Jesus to the story he tells us, through his life, ministry, death and resurrection, can bring us back in touch with God's constant and unwavering love for us all:

> In order to be capable of mercy, therefore, we must first of all dispose ourselves to listen to the Word of God. This means rediscovering the value of silence in order to meditate on the Word that comes to us. In this way, it will be possible to contemplate God's mercy and adopt it as our lifestyle. (*Misericordiae vultus*, 13)

Merciful Father
A Prayer for the Year of Mercy

Merciful Father,
Lord of heaven and earth,
we give you thanks for your tender mercy
and sweet loving-kindness,
 revealed in the face of Jesus, your Son.
  By the gift of your Holy Spirit,
   may we be blessed, with Jesus
    in your warm embrace,
     even when we have to carry the cross of suffering
     and pain.
      By the grace of the Spirit
       may we grow to know more fully your everlasting
       love,
        and love you always, and our neighbour,
        learning to receive forgiveness and give
        forgiveness.
        Through the watchful care of Jesus Christ,
         our gentle shepherd and Risen Saviour,
        may we keep our hearts always open
       to those whom we love and to all in need,
      compassionate as you are compassionate.
May his healing peace touch us, and all those we meet,
so that we may experience even now,
the coming Kingdom of your love and mercy,
with Christ,
with Mary, his beloved mother, and our mother too,
with all the angels and saints, one in communion and
mission,
through the same Christ our Lord. Amen.

Gareth Byrne

The Lord is My Shepherd

The Lord is my shepherd;
there is nothing I shall want.
Fresh and green are the pastures
where he gives me repose.
Near restful waters he leads me,
to revive my drooping spirit.

He guides me along the right
path;
he is true to his name.
If I should walk in the valley of
darkness
no evil would I fear.
You are there with your crook and
your staff;

with these you give me comfort.
You have prepared a banquet for
me
in the sight of my foes.
My head you have anointed with
oil;
my cup is overflowing.

Surely goodness and kindness shall
follow me
all the days of my life.
In the Lord's own house shall I
dwell
for ever and ever. Amen.

Psalm 22 (23)

A Father Who Never Gives Up

So he set off and went to his father. While he was still far off, his father saw him and was filled with compassion; he ran and put his arms around him and kissed him. Then the son said to him, 'Father, I have sinned against heaven and before you; I am no longer worthy to be called your son.' But the father said to his servants, 'Quickly, bring out a robe – the best one – and put it on him; put a ring on his finger and sandals on his feet. And get the fatted calf and kill it, and let us eat and celebrate; for this son of mine was dead and is alive again; he was lost and is found!' and they began to celebrate.

Luke 15:20-24

Unless we mourn properly our hurts, our losses, life's unfairness, our shattered dreams … and all the life that we once had but that has now passed us by, we will live either in an unhealthy fantasy or an ever-intensifying bitterness. Spiritually we see this in the older brother of the prodigal son. His bitterness and inability to dance points to what he is still clinging to – life's unfairness, his own hurt, and his unfulfilled fantasies. He is living in his father's house but he is no longer receiving the spirit of that house.

Ronald Rolheiser

In the parables devoted to mercy, Jesus reveals the nature of God as that of a Father who never gives up until he has forgiven the wrong and overcome rejection with compassion and mercy.

Francis, *Misericordiae vultus*, 9

A Prayer to own your Beauty

O God
help me
to believe
the truth about myself
no matter
how beautiful it is!

Macrina Wiederkehr

May I accept my past,
may I accept my
present,
may I accept my future,
may I have the wisdom
and courage
to humbly accept
God's will in my
history.

Wayne Simsic

**All it takes is one
good person to
restore hope.**

Francis, *Laudato Si'*, 71

Consult not your Fears

Consult not your fears but your hopes and your dreams.
Think not about your frustrations, but about your unfulfilled potential.
Concern yourself not with what you tried and failed in, but with what
it is still possible for you to do.

St John XXIII

Religion for Christians is not a 'blind search for God'. It is a
relationship, a response of faith to God revealed to us in human history
and in our times too. God reaches out to us in all our ups and downs,
calling each person into ongoing and deepening conversion. We are
invited to know and love God and to allow God's grace to shape our
lives. We too can grow into a relationship of intimate love with God.

Share the Good News, 26

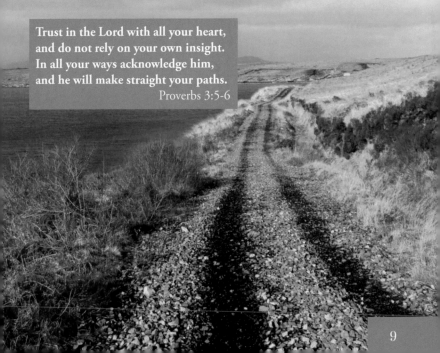

Trust in the Lord with all your heart,
and do not rely on your own insight.
In all your ways acknowledge him,
and he will make straight your paths.
Proverbs 3:5-6

I Cannot Keep Silent

I cannot be silent then, nor indeed should I, about the great benefits and grace which the Lord saw fit to confer on me in my captivity …
This much I know for sure. Before I had to suffer I was like a stone lying in the deep mud. Then he who is mighty came and in his mercy he not only pulled me out but lifted me up and placed me at the very top of the wall …
I give thanks to God tirelessly who kept me faithful in the day of trial, so that today I offer sacrifice to him confidently, the living sacrifice of my life to Christ, my Lord, who preserves me in all my troubles. I can say therefore: Who am I, Lord, and what is my calling that you should cooperate with me with such divine power?
… I praise and proclaim your name in all places, not only when things go well but also in times of stress. Whether I receive good or ill, I return thanks equally to God, who taught me always to trust him unreservedly.

St Patrick, *Confessions*

Lord, have mercy,
Christ, have mercy,
Lord, have mercy.

A Thiarna, déan trócaire,
A Chríost, déan trócaire,
A Thiarna, déan trócaire.

From the Heart of the Trinity

From the heart of the Trinity, from
the depths of the mystery of God,
the great river of mercy wells up and
overflows unceasingly. It is a spring
that will never run dry, no matter
how many people draw from it. Every
time someone is in need, he or she can
approach it, because the mercy of God
never ends.

Misericordiae vultus, 22

I bind unto myself today
the strong name of the Trinity,
by invocation of the same,
the Three in One, the One in Three.
I bind this day to me for ever,
by power of faith, Christ's Incarnation;
His baptism in the Jordan river;
His death on the Cross for my
salvation;
His bursting from the spicèd tomb;
His riding on the heavenly way;
His coming at the day of doom;
I bind unto myself today.

St Patrick's Breastplate

So if anyone is in Christ, there is a new
creation: everything old has passed
away; see everything has become new.

1 Corinthians 5:17

Everything in Him Speaks of Mercy

No one can place limits on the love of God who is ever ready to forgive.

Everything in him speaks of mercy. Nothing in him is devoid of compassion.

Above all let us listen to the words of Jesus who made mercy an ideal of life and a criterion for the credibility of our faith.

Mercy is the force that reawakens us to new life and instils in us the courage to look to the future with hope.

Misericordiae vultus, 3, 8, 9, 10

Be merciful, just as your Father is merciful.
Do not judge, and you will not be judged; do not condemn, and you will not be condemned.
Forgive and you will be forgiven; give and it will be given to you.
A good measure, pressed down, shaken together, running over, will be put into your lap;
for the measure you give will be the measure you get back.

Luke 6:36-38

The Benedictus

Blessed be the Lord, the God of Israel!
He has visited his people and redeemed
them.
He has raised up for us a mighty saviour
in the house of David his servant,
as he promised by the lips of holy men,
those who were his prophets from of old.
A saviour who would free us from our foes,
from the hands of all who hate us.
So his love for our fathers is fulfilled
and his holy covenant remembered.
He swore to Abraham our father to grant
us,
that free from fear, and saved from the
hands of our foes,
we might serve him in holiness and justice
all the days of our life in his presence.
As for you, little child,
you shall be called a prophet of God, the
Most High.
You shall go ahead of the Lord
to prepare his ways before him.
To make known to his people their
salvation
through forgiveness of all their sins,
the loving-kindness of the heart of our
God
who visits us like the dawn from on high.
He will give light to those in darkness,
those who dwell in the shadow of death,
and guide us into the way of peace.

Luke 1:68-79

I Have Loved you with an Everlasting Love

O Lord you have enticed me,
and I have let myself be enticed;
you have overpowered me,
and you have prevailed …
If I say, 'I must not mention him,
or speak any more in his name',
then within me there is something
like a burning fire
shut up in my bones;
I am weary with holding it in, and I
cannot.

Jeremiah 20:7, 9

**I have loved you with an
everlasting love;
therefore I have continued
my faithfulness to you.**

Jeremiah 31:3

To Love and to Love Deeply

Do not be afraid to love and to love deeply. You might be afraid of the pain that deep love can cause. When those you love deeply reject you, leave you, or die, your heart will be broken. But that should not hold you back from loving deeply. The pain that comes from deep love makes your love ever more fruitful. It is like the plough that breaks the ground to allow the seed to take root and grow into a strong plant. Every time you experience the pain of rejection, absence, or death, you are faced with a choice. You can become bitter, decide not to love again, or you can stand straight in your pain and let the soil on which you stand become richer and more able to give life to new seeds. The more you have loved and allowed yourself to suffer because of your love, the more you will be able to let your heart grow wider and deeper. When your love is truly giving and receiving, those whom you love will not leave your heart even when they depart from you. They will become part of yourself and thus gradually build a community within you. Those you have deeply loved become part of you.

Henri Nouwen

15

He Has Spoken to us by a Son

After God had spoken many times and in various ways through the prophets, 'in these last days he has spoken to us by a Son' (Heb 1:1-2). For he sent his Son, the eternal Word who enlightens all humankind, to live among them and tell them about the inner life of God.

Vatican II, *Dei verbum*, 4

It is the Father's will that we should recognise Christ as our brother in the persons of all men and women and should love them with an active love, in word and in deed, thus bearing witness to the truth; and it is his will that we should share with others the mystery of his heavenly love. In this way people all over the world will awaken to a lively hope, the gift of the Holy Spirit, that they will one day be admitted to the haven of surpassing peace and happiness in their homeland radiant with the glory of the Lord.

Vatican II, *Gaudium et spes*, 93

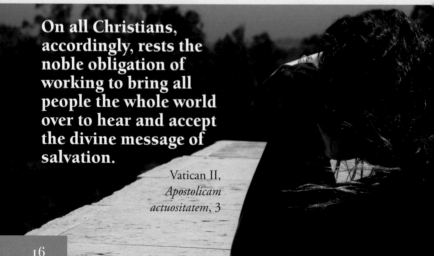

On all Christians, accordingly, rests the noble obligation of working to bring all people the whole world over to hear and accept the divine message of salvation.

Vatican II,
Apostolicam actuositatem, 3

The Wonder of Prayer

**The wonder of prayer is revealed beside the
well where we come seeking water: there,
Christ comes to meet every human being. It is
he who first seeks us and asks us for a drink.
Jesus thirsts; his asking arises from the depths
of God's desire for us. Whether we realise it
or not, prayer is the encounter of God's thirst
with ours. God thirsts that we may thirst for
him.**

Catechism of the Catholic Church, 2560

I implore you, good Jesus,
that as in your mercy you
have given me
to drink in with delight the
words of your knowledge,
so of your loving kindness
you will also grant me one
day to come to you,
the fountain of wisdom,
and stand for ever before
your face.

The Venerable Bede (673–735)

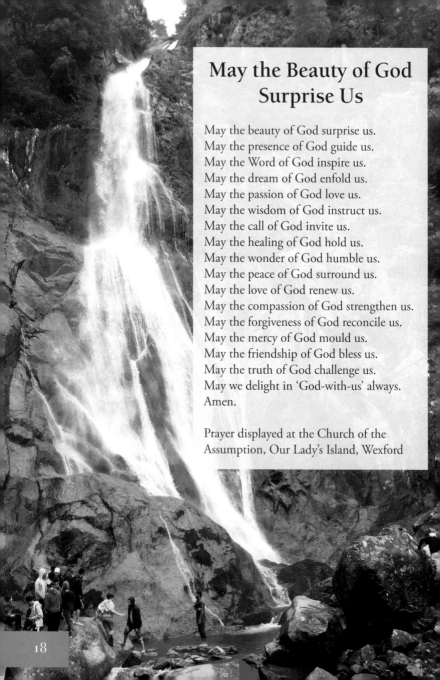

May the Beauty of God Surprise Us

May the beauty of God surprise us.
May the presence of God guide us.
May the Word of God inspire us.
May the dream of God enfold us.
May the passion of God love us.
May the wisdom of God instruct us.
May the call of God invite us.
May the healing of God hold us.
May the wonder of God humble us.
May the peace of God surround us.
May the love of God renew us.
May the compassion of God strengthen us.
May the forgiveness of God reconcile us.
May the mercy of God mould us.
May the friendship of God bless us.
May the truth of God challenge us.
May we delight in 'God-with-us' always.
Amen.

Prayer displayed at the Church of the
Assumption, Our Lady's Island, Wexford

I Have Called you by Name

But now thus says the Lord,
he who created you, O Jacob,
he who formed you, O Israel:
Do not fear, for I have
redeemed you;
I have called you by name, you
are mine.
When you pass through the
waters, I will be with you;
and through the rivers, they
shall not overwhelm you;
when you walk through fire you
shall not be burned,
and the flame shall not
consume you.
For I am the Lord your God,
The Holy One of Israel, your
Saviour …
you are precious in my sight,
and honoured and I love you …
Do not fear, I am with you.

Isaiah 43:1-5

**Draw near to God
and he will draw
near to you.**

James 4:8a

The Lord's Prayer

Our Father
Who art in heaven
Hallowed be thy name
Thy kingdom come
Thy will be done
On earth as it is in heaven
Give us this day our daily bread
And forgive us our trespasses
As we forgive those who trespass
against us
And lead us not into temptation
But deliver us from evil.
Amen.

Like the Deer that Yearns for Running Streams

Like the deer that yearns for running streams,
so my soul is yearning for you my God.
My soul is thirsting for God, the God of my life;
when can I enter and see the face of God?
My tears have become my bread, by night, by day,
as I hear it said all day long, 'Where is your God?' …
Why are you cast down my soul, why groan within me?
Hope in God; I will praise him still,
my saviour and my God …
Deep is calling on deep, in the roar of waters:
your torrents and all your waves swept over me.
By day the Lord will send his loving kindness;
by night I will sing to him, praise the God of my life.
I will say to God, my rock: 'Why have you forgotten me?
Why do I go mourning oppressed by the foe?'
With cries that pierce me to the heart, my enemies revile me,
saying to me all day long: 'Where is your God?'
Why are you cast down my soul, why groan within me?
Hope in God; I will praise him still,
my saviour and my God.

Psalm 41 (42)

Sing to me your Joyful Song

O sweet and loving
God,
when I stay asleep
too long,
oblivious to all your
many blessings,
then, please wake
me up,
and sing to me your
joyful song.
It is a song without
noise or notes.
It is a song of love
beyond all telling.
I can hear it in
my soul when you
awaken me
to your presence.

Mechthild of Magdeburg
(1210–80)

Love one Another as I Have Loved you

Jesus said: 'This is my commandment, that you love one another as I have loved you. No one has greater love than this, to lay down one's life for one's friends. You are my friends if you do what I command you. I do not call you servants any longer, because the servant does not know what the master is doing; but I called you friends, because I have made known to you everything that I have heard from my Father. You did not choose me but I chose you. And I appointed you to go and bear fruit, fruit that will last, so that the Father will give you whatever you ask him in my name. I am giving you these commands so that you may love one another.'

John 15:12-17

At the Cross of Jesus

When Jesus saw his mother and the disciple whom he loved standing beside her, he said to his mother, 'Woman, here is your son.' Then he said to the disciple, 'Here is your mother.' And from that hour the disciple took her into his own home.

John 19:25-27

'My God,
my God,
why have you
forsaken me?'

Matthew 27:46

'Father, forgive them;
for they do not know what
they are doing.'

Luke 23:34

Then Jesus, crying with a loud
voice, said, 'Father, into your
hands I commend my spirit.'

Luke 23:46

Now when the centurion, who
stood facing him, saw that in
this way he breathed his last,
he said, 'Truly this man was
God's Son!'

Mark 15:39

You are the Source
of all Love

Lord,
You are the source of all love.
You showed it through Jesus
who shed his blood for us.
We ask you: open our hearts,
make them as generous as yours.
Give us a heart eager to serve others.
Let us be the expression
of your smile on the world.
Amen.

> Prayer associated with the Basilica of
> the Precious Blood, Bruges

May the God of new beginnings lead
us forward this day.
May the God who brought us to new
life in Christ
fill us will resurrection joy this day.
May the God who abides within us
be revealed to all we meet this day.
May the God who consoles and
protects us,
sooth any heartache this day.
May the God who desires abundance
of life for all creation
renew our spirits this day.
Amen! Alleluia!

> Anon

The Stations of the Cross

The Stations of the Cross in our parish church aid us as we walk with Jesus through his Passion and Death. We can, however, meditate on the Stations of the Cross, out walking, while sitting at home, wherever we are, remembering Christ's sacrifice on the Cross for us.

Name each particular Station and pray the verse below. Give yourself some quiet time with Christ in that moment of his Passion. Remember then a loved one, a person who has asked you for prayers, those who do not have all they require. Ask the Lord, maybe, for a gift you need yourself or for the ability to respond generously to others. Pray an Our Father, a Hail Mary and a Glory Be to the Father, asking that God's love and mercy be poured out upon you and on those you have remembered in prayer. Then move on to the next Station in your own time.

We adore you, O Christ, and we bless you, because by your holy Cross, you have redeemed the world.

1. Jesus is condemned to death
2. Jesus carries his cross
3. Jesus falls the first time
4. Jesus meets his mother
5. Simon of Cyrene helps Jesus carry the cross
6. Veronica wipes the face of Jesus
7. Jesus falls the second time
8. Jesus meets the women of Jerusalem
9. Jesus falls the third time
10. Jesus is stripped of his garments
11. Jesus is nailed to the cross
12. Jesus dies on the cross
13. Jesus is taken down from the cross
14. Jesus is laid in the tomb

Eternity is not what happens at the end of time, after we are dead. Every time we love and forgive then we have put a foot into eternity, which is God's life. And that is why we can be joyful even on Good Friday, even in the face of suffering and death.

Timothy Radcliffe

Take Lord, Receive

Take Lord, receive
all my liberty
my memory, understanding
my entire will.
Give me only your love and your grace,
that's enough for me.
Your love and your grace are enough for me.

Take Lord, receive
all I have and possess.
You have given all to me.
Now I return it.
Give me only your love and your grace,
that's enough for me.
Your love and your grace are enough for me.

Take Lord, receive.
All is yours now.
Dispose of it
wholly according to your will.
Give me only your love and your grace,
that's enough for me.
Your love and your grace are enough for me.

Prayer of St Ignatius, version by John Foley

27

The Comfort of Others

Companion of the Suffering,
the touch of your embrace
comes to me in the gift
of those who stand with me.
How grateful I am
for the compassionate ones
who wrap me in their care,
and console me with their
kindness.

Source of all Love,
what encouragement is mine
in those you have given me.
Thank you for their
thoughtfulness,
their patience, their empathy.
When they stand with me,
I know in a certain way
that you have not abandoned
me.

Joyce Rupp

Christian Love is Deliberate, it is Chosen

The deepest act of faith is not in the reality that God exists but in the reality that he loves me, knows my name, that I have the power of his heart, his compassion within myself. But I will never discover this unless I exercise it. Select a person who is in and out of your life and decide to love him. Christian love does not consist in finding an object that draws love from you. Christian friendship is not an accident of finding the right chemistry. Christian love is deliberate, it is chosen. I love this person not because he is worthy of my love but because I have the capacity to love and to call to life, to create. No one of us will ever appreciate the power we have to give life to one another. We are the image of God because we have the power to believe in someone. We have the power to create life in him. There's no greater gift which we can give to another person than our time, our presence. Every person has a capacity to bring us into a new room within ourselves which has never been opened before.

Edward J. Farrell

Called to Mission, Sharing the Gift of Christ

The Christian today, graced by the Holy Spirit, is the bearer, too, of this life-giving, dynamic and transforming presence, Jesus Christ, who calls us to live our lives inspired by his life, his truth, his way. We are never alone. Jesus brings us beyond ourselves into a whole new world of loving relationship with God, with our neighbour, with our community, with society and with all of creation: 'Union with Christ is also union with all those to whom he gives himself.' Because Jesus is good news, the Christian today, and the Christian community, can be good news too, called to mission, sharing the gift of Christ, carrying hope into a world that seeks continuously to know, to understand, to live fully and to love.

Share the Good News, 8

Go out and proclaim the merciful embrace of the Father. Go out to those who are burdened by pain and failure, who feel that their lives are empty, and proclaim the folly of a loving Father who wants to anoint them with the oil of hope, the oil of salvation … Go out with the ointment that soothes wounds and heals hearts … Mission is always the fruit of a life which knows what it is to be found and healed, encountered and forgiven.

Francis, Homily at the Canonisation Mass of Junipero Serra

A Samaritan while travelling came near him; and when he saw him, he was moved by pity. He went to him and bandaged his wounds, having poured oil and wine on them.

Luke 10:34

Prayer of Pope Francis for the Extraordinary Jubilee of Mercy

Lord Jesus Christ,
you have taught us to be merciful like the heavenly Father,
and have told us that whoever sees you sees Him.
Show us your face and we will be saved.
Your loving gaze freed Zacchaeus and Matthew from being
enslaved by money;
the adulteress and Magdalene from seeking happiness only in
created things;
made Peter weep after his betrayal,
and assured Paradise to the repentant thief.
Let us hear, as if addressed to each one of us, the words that you
spoke to the Samaritan woman:
'If you knew the gift of God!'
You are the visible face of the invisible Father,
of the God who manifests his power above all by forgiveness and
mercy:
let the Church be your visible face in the world, its Lord risen and
glorified.
You willed that your ministers would also be clothed in weakness
in order that they may feel compassion for those in ignorance and
error:
let everyone who approaches them feel sought after, loved, and
forgiven by God.
Send your Spirit and consecrate every one of us with its anointing,
so that the Jubilee of Mercy may be a year of grace from the Lord,
and your Church, with renewed enthusiasm, may bring good news
to the poor,
proclaim liberty to captives and the oppressed,
and restore sight to the blind.
We ask this through the intercession of Mary, Mother of Mercy,
you who live and reign with the Father and the Holy Spirit for ever
and ever.
Amen.

The Ministry of Compassion and Healing

Jesus sent his disciples out to care for the sick, and by so doing to participate in his ministry of compassion and healing. From the beginning, Christians have put care of the sick high on their agenda, knowing that in this they are serving Christ himself.

Share the Good News, 55

Anointing of the Sick
Through this holy anointing
may the Lord in his love and mercy
help you with the grace of the Holy Spirit.
May the Lord who frees you from sin
save you and raise you up.
Amen.

Ritual for the Anointing of the Sick

Lord Jesus heal me.
Heal in me whatever you see needs healing.
Heal me of whatever might separate me
from you.
Heal my memory, heal my heart, heal my
emotions,
heal my spirit, heal my body, heal my soul.
Lay your hands gently upon me
and heal me through your love for me.
Amen.

Anon

Holy Spirit, Giver of all Life

Holy Spirit,
giving life to all life,
moving all creatures,
root of all things,
washing them clean,
wiping out their mistakes,
healing their wounds,
you are our true life,
luminous, wonderful,
awakening the heart from its
ancient sleep.

Hildegard of Bingen
(1098–1179)

Holy Spirit, Lord of Light,
how gently and lovingly
you wake in my heart,
where in secret you dwell alone;
and in your sweet breathing,
filled with good and glory,
how tenderly you swell my heart
with love.
Come then, Father of the poor,
Come with treasures that endure.

Gareth Byrne
Based on the Pentecost Sequence
and a prayer by St John of the
Cross

33

The Work of Healing and Salvation

The Lord Jesus Christ, physician of our souls and bodies, who forgave the sins of the paralytic and restored him to bodily health, has willed that his Church continue, in the power of the Holy Spirit, his work of healing and salvation, even among her own members.

Catechism of the Catholic Church, 1421

The steadfast love of the Lord never ceases, his mercies never come to an end; They are new every morning; great is your faithfulness … The Lord is good to those who wait for him, to the soul that seeks him. It is good that one should wait quietly for the salvation of the Lord.

Lamentations 3:22-23, 25-26

God of all embracing love, praise and glory to you for the many ways you show your love in my life. Send your Holy Spirit into my heart so that I may accept your gifts of forgiveness and healing, that my whole being may sing your praises and that all around me may know the wonders of your love. Take away from me all guilt, anxiety and fear so that I can bask in the knowledge of you and rest in your loving arms. I ask this in the name of Jesus your beloved Son. Amen.

Johnny Doherty

Peace be with You

When it was evening on that day, the first day of the week, and the doors of the house where the disciples had met were locked for fear of the Jews, Jesus came and stood among them and said, 'Peace be with you.' After he said this, he showed them his hands and his side. Then the disciples rejoiced when they saw the Lord. Jesus said to them again, 'Peace be with you. As the Father has sent me, so I send you.' When he had said this, he breathed on them and said to them, 'Receive the Holy Spirit. If you forgive the sins of any, they are forgiven them; if you retain the sins of any, they are retained.'

John 20:19-23

When the fact of being loved by God is experienced, understood and cherished by the person, efforts to explain the teaching of Jesus Christ and the challenge he presents us with make sense in a whole new way. The Church's ongoing endeavour to know and love Christ, following as disciples in his footsteps toward the full realisation of God's Kingdom, becomes a way of life that is fully and personally embraced.

Share the Good News, 25

The Earthly Healing Hands of the Heavenly, Risen Lord

Through the sacraments, Christ himself touches, strengthens, heals us. The sacraments are, so to speak, the earthly hands of the heavenly, risen Lord. What he touches is healed.

Christ does not heal by simply taking away the symptoms of the illness. His healing goes to the depths … His healing goes to the roots of all that is unhealthy: the sin that separates from God, the source of life. That is why the healing element of the forgiveness of sins is part of every sacrament. We are really healthy only when we are reconciled with God, united with Christ, and filled with the Holy Spirit …

The more we recognise in faith the Church herself as the sacrament of God's love, the more the healing dimension of the sacraments will open itself up to us. She is healing fellowship, loving Mother, who dispenses the 'medicine' of Christ to us.

Christoph Schönborn

Do not grieve the Holy Spirit of God, with which you were marked with a seal for the day of redemption. Put away from you all bitterness and wrath and anger and wrangling and slander, together with malice, and be kind to one another, as God in Christ has forgiven you. Therefore be imitators of God, as beloved children, and live in love, as Christ loved us and gave himself up for us, a fragrant offering and sacrifice to God.

Ephesians, 4:30–5:2

The Sacrament of Penance and Reconciliation

Act of Sorrow

O my God, I thank you for loving me.
I am sorry for my sins
For not loving others
and not loving you.
Help me to live like Jesus and not sin again.
Amen.

Words of Absolution

God, the Father of mercies,
through the death and resurrection of his
Son
has reconciled the world to himself
and sent the Holy Spirit among us
for the forgiveness of sins;
through the ministry of the Church
may God give you pardon and peace,
and I absolve you from your sins
in the name of the Father, and of the Son,
and of the Holy Spirit.
Amen.

Rite of Penance

To Bring Forgiveness to the World

Jesus gifted the disciples with peace and joy, sending them as the
Father had sent him, to bring forgiveness into the world (Jn 20:19-23).
The Church should be a sign and instrument of that forgiveness and
reconciliation. The sacrament of Penance and Reconciliation celebrates
Christ's forgiveness of us and his healing of our hearts and minds. By
confessing, we take responsibility for our sin, recognising it for what it
is. Our sorrow for what we have done, or what we failed to do, leads
to contrition, absolution, penance and renewed hope. We can act
differently, and pledge ourselves so to do. We open ourselves in Jesus
Christ to reconciliation with God and with one another.

Share the Good News, 55

While all the Sacraments bring us an experience of the mercy that comes
from Christ's dying and rising, it is the Sacrament of Reconciliation that is
the unique Sacrament of mercy.

Irish Catholic Catechism for Adults, p. 271

It must be recalled … this reconciliation with God leads, as it were, to
other reconciliations, which repair the other breaches caused by sin. The
forgiven penitent is reconciled with himself in his inmost being, where
he regains his innermost truth. He is reconciled with his brethren whom
he has in some way offended and wounded. He is reconciled with the
Church. He is reconciled with all creation.

St John Paul II, *Reconciliatio et paenitentia*, 31

All Need God's Mercy

It should be fairly obvious that becoming more aware of our own need for conversion and forgiveness makes it more difficult to take a condemning or judgemental stance. If we are all sinners, no one has a right to sit in judgment on another. All need God's mercy, and no one really has a superior position … The more we recognise who we are before God, the more we will become a forgiving community that truly welcomes sinners to reconciliation.

Christoph Schönborn

Personal behaviour is fully human when it is born of love, manifests love and is ordered by love.

Compendium of the Social Doctrine of the Church, 583

Lord, show me your mercy
and make my heart glad.
I am like the man going to Jericho
wounded by robbers:
Good Samaritan, come help me.
I am like the sheep gone astray:
Good Shepherd, come seek me
and bring me home safe.
Let me dwell in your house all my days
and praise you forever.
Amen.

St Jerome (340–420)

With Judaism, Islam and Other Noble Religious Traditions

There is an aspect of mercy that goes beyond the confines of the Church. It relates us to Judaism and Islam, both of which consider mercy to be one of God's most important attributes. Israel was the first to receive this revelation which continues in history as the source of an inexhaustible richness meant to be shared with all mankind … The pages of the Old Testament are steeped in mercy, because they narrate the works that the Lord performed in favour of his people at the most trying moments in their history. Among the privileged names that Islam attributes to the Creator are 'Merciful and Kind'. This invocation is often on the lips of faithful Muslims who feel themselves accompanied and sustained by mercy in their daily weakness. They too believe that no one can place a limit on divine mercy because its door is always open.

I trust that this Jubilee Year celebrating the mercy of God will foster an encounter with these religions and with other noble religious traditions; may it open us to even more fervent dialogue so that we might know and understand one another better; may it eliminate every form of closed-mindedness and disrespect, and drive out every form of violence and discrimination.

Misericordiae vultus, 23

An Oasis of Mercy

The Church's first truth is the love of Christ. The Church makes herself a servant of this love and mediates it to all people: a love that forgives and expresses itself in the gift of oneself. Consequently, wherever the Church is present, the mercy of the Father must be evident, in our parishes, communities, associations and movements, in a word, wherever there are Christians, everyone should find an oasis of mercy.

Misericordiae vultus,12

Lord Jesus Christ,
who said to your Apostles:
Peace I leave you, my peace I give you,
look not on our sins,
but on the faith of your Church,
and graciously grant her peace and unity
in accordance with your will.
Who live and reign for ever and ever.
Amen.

Peace Prayer at Mass

Peace cannot be achieved on earth unless people's welfare is safeguarded and people freely and in a spirit of mutual trust share with one another the riches of their minds and their talents. A firm determination to respect the dignity of other individuals and peoples along with the deliberate practice of friendliness are absolutely necessary for the achievement of peace. Accordingly, peace is also the fruit of love, for love goes beyond what justice can achieve.

Vatican II, *Gaudium et spes*, 78

Jesus, Lamb of God, You Take Away the Sins of the World

Jesus, Lamb of God, you take away
the sins of the world:
have mercy on us.
Jesus, Bread of Life, you take away
the sins of the world:
have mercy on us.
Jesus, Prince of Peace, you take away
the sins of the world:
have mercy on us.
Jesus, Word of God, you take away
the sins of the world:
have mercy on us.
Jesus, Tree of Life, you take away the
sins of the world:
have mercy on us.

Jesus, Lord of Lords, you take away
the sins of the world:
have mercy on us.
Jesus, Fire of Love, you take away
the sins of the world:
have mercy on us.
Jesus, Bread of Peace, you take away
the sins of the world:
have mercy on us.
Jesus, Hope of all, you take away the
sins of the world:
have mercy on us.
Jesus, Lamb of God, you take away
the sins of the world:
grant us your peace.

Marty Haugen

A Uain Dé, a thógann
peacaí an domhain,
déan trócaire orainn.

A Uain Dé, a thógann
peacaí an domhain,
déan trócaire orainn.

A Uain Dé, a thógann
peacaí an domhain,
tabhair dúinn
síocháin.

New Birth into a Living Hope

Blessed be the God and Father of our Lord Jesus Christ! By his great mercy he has given us a new birth into a living hope through the resurrection of Jesus from the dead, and into an inheritance that is imperishable, undefiled, and unfading, kept in heaven for you, who are being protected by the power of God through faith for a salvation ready to be revealed in the last time. In this you rejoice, even if now for a little while you have had to suffer various trials, so that the genuineness of your faith – being more precious than gold that, though perishable, is tested by fire – may be found to result in praise and glory and honour when Jesus Christ is revealed. Although you have not seen him, you love him; and even though you do not see him now, you believe in him and rejoice with an indescribable and glorious joy, for you are receiving the outcome of your faith, the salvation of your souls.

1 Peter 1:3-9

If you were not risen,
Lord Christ, to whom would we go
to discover a radiance
of the face of God.
If you were not risen,
we would not be together
seeking your communion.
We would not find in your presence
forgiveness,
wellspring of a new beginning.
If you were not risen,
where would we draw the energy
for following you
right to the end of our existence,
for choosing you again and anew?

Brother Roger of Taizé

The Great Parade of all God's Creatures

For Catholic spirituality, much of what ecological consciousness calls to mind pivots around sacramentality. When people consider God's creation with eyes of faith, they see sacraments – material signs of grace – everywhere. The sacramental materials featured in the primary Catholic rituals – bread, wine, water, oil – are the most prominent, but a little imagination makes it clear that in principle everything made by God refers beyond itself, to its source. So wax, incense, flowers, music, painting, wheat, cotton, palm branches, baby chicks – all carry a lesson. The lesson need not be articulate. It is enough for people to open their hearts to all the good things that come from their Father of Lights. When they do so, they see creation as a cornucopia – a never-failing stream. As well, they see why the Word of God was willing to take flesh and join the great parade of all God's creatures.

John T. Carmody

To sense each creature singing the hymn of its existence is to live joyfully in God's love and hope.
Catholic Bishops' Conference of Japan

Praised Be You:
Laudato Si'

The Spirit of God has filled the universe with possibilities and therefore, from the very heart of things, something new can always emerge.

Creation can only be understood as a gift from the outstretched hand of the Father of all, and a reality illuminated by the love which calls us together into universal communion.

The entire material universe speaks of God's love, his boundless affection for us. Soil, water, mountains: everything is as it were a caress of God. The history of our friendship with God is always linked to particular places which take on an intensely personal meaning; we remember places, and revisiting those memories does us much good ... going back to these places is a chance to recover something of our true selves.

A sense of deep communion with the rest of nature cannot be real if our hearts lack tenderness, compassion and concern for our fellow human beings.

Laudato Si', 76, 80, 84, 91

Called to Communion with God

Human dignity rests above all on the fact that humanity is called to communion with God. The invitation to converse with God is addressed to men and women as soon as they are born. For if people exist it is because God has created them through love, and through love continues to keep them in existence. They cannot live fully in the truth unless they freely acknowledge that love and entrust themselves to their creator.

Vatican II, *Gaudium et spes*, 19

Meanwhile, everybody remains a question to themselves, one that is dimly perceived and left unanswered. For there are times, especially in the major events of life, when nobody can altogether escape from such self-questioning. God alone, who calls people to deeper thought and more humble probing, can fully and with complete certainty supply an answer to this questioning.

Vatican II, *Gaudium et spes*, 21

God's Spirit poured into the human heart – the Prophets proclaim – will make these same sentiments of justice and solidarity, which reside in the Lord's heart, take root in you (see Jeremiah 31:33 and Ezekiel 36:26-27).

Compendium of the Social Doctrine of the Church, 25

Moved by the Fragility, Weakness and Suffering of the Other

Compassion may be understood as the capacity to be attracted and moved by the fragility, weakness, and suffering of another. It is the ability to be vulnerable enough to undergo risk and loss for the good of the other. Compassion involves a movement to be of assistance to the other … a movement of participation in the experience of the other in order to be present and available in solidarity and communion. Compassion requires sensitivity to what is weak and/or wounded, as well as the vulnerability to be affected by the other. It also demands action to alleviate pain and suffering. One's deepest inner feelings should always lead to outward compassionate acts of mercy and kindness.

Michael Downey

Christians can repeat in an individual way the words of Jesus: The Spirit of the Lord is upon me, because he has anointed me to preach good news to the poor. He has sent me to proclaim release to the captives and recovery of sight to the blind, to set at liberty those who are oppressed, to proclaim the acceptable year of the Lord (Luke 4:18-19; cf. Isaiah 61:1-2). Thus with the outpouring of the Holy Spirit in Baptism and Confirmation, the baptised share in the same mission of Jesus as the Christ, the Saviour-Messiah.

St John Paul II, Christifideles laici, 13

Love 'makes one see in neighbour another self'.

Vatican II, *Gaudium et spes*, 78

O Lord, Open my Eyes

O Lord, open my eyes that I may see the need of others,
open my ears that I may hear their cries,
open my heart so that they need not be without succour.
Let me not be afraid to defend the weak
because of the anger of the strong,
nor afraid to defend the poor
because of the anger of the rich.
Show me where love and hope and faith are needed,
and use me to bring them to these places.
Open my eyes and ears
that I may, this coming day,
be able to do some work of peace for thee.

Alan Paton

**Always be the first to love
and be faithful to love
even if you get no answer.
Don't make conditions.
Be thankful and praise God
when you realise you are loved.**

Rule for a New Brother

The Works of Mercy

The works of mercy are charitable actions by which we come to the aid of our neighbour in his spiritual and bodily necessities. Instructing, advising, consoling, comforting, are spiritual works of mercy, as are forgiving and bearing wrongs patiently. The corporal works of mercy consist especially in feeding the hungry, sheltering the homeless, clothing the naked, visiting the sick and imprisoned, and burying the dead. Among these, giving alms to the poor is one of the chief witnesses to fraternal charity: it is also a work of justice pleasing to God.

Catechism of the Catholic Church, 2447

Then the king will say to those on his right hand,
'Come you that are blessed by my Father,
inherit the kingdom prepared for you from the foundation of the world;
for I was hungry and you gave me food,
I was thirsty and you gave me something to drink,
I was a stranger and you welcomed me,
I was naked and you gave me clothing,
I was sick and you took care of me,
I was in prison and you visited me.'

Then the righteous will answer him,
'Lord, when was it we saw you hungry and gave you food,
or thirsty and gave you something to drink?
And when was it that we saw you a stranger and welcomed you,
or naked and gave you clothing?
And when was it we saw you sick or in prison and visited you?'
And the king will answer them,
'Truly I tell you,
just as you did it to one of the least of these
who are members of my family, you did it to me.'

Matthew 25:34-40

Strengthen the Young

God our Father,
strengthen the young
in our unsteady world,
to love what is good
and rejoice in what is right.

Victor Hoagland

... **the future of humanity rests with people who are capable of providing the generations to come with reasons for living and for hope.**

Vatican II, *Gaudium et spes*, 31

When adults help young people discover the root of their emotions, they help them discover and understand what is sacred: truth, love, loyalty, authenticity, respect, fairness, integrity, virtue, peace and compassion.

Michael Carotta

from Glory on the Face of Christ

… God entrusts
the love and care he has for the
world
to the lives of his people.
Each one of us
is a space for the Spirit to inhabit,
a place for the Father to live,
a face on which the light of Jesus
shines.

As a river carries water, we carry
God,
as the sun carries light, we shine
out God,
as a face mirrors a personality, we
mirror God.
This is the glory of God,
Father, Son and Holy Spirit,
the one who is mother and father
of us all,
and gives life to all,
the one who is saviour and friend
and brings wholeness,
the one who is peace and courage
and brings conviction.

Donal Neary

me in the mirror

Be Blessed

Be dependent on God, and blessed!
Be mindful of those who have died, and be blessed!
Be close to the earth, and be blessed!
Be just and fair, and be blessed!
Be compassionate, and be blessed!
Be genuine and true, and be blessed!
Be a peacemaker, and be blessed!
Be prepared to stand up for what is right, and be blessed!

Alive-O 7, Teacher's Book

God's very being is love. By sending his only Son and the Spirit of Love in the fullness of time, God has revealed his innermost secret: God himself is an eternal exchange of love, Father, Son and Holy Spirit, and he has destined us to share in that exchange.

Catechism of the Catholic Church, 221

Communion with all People

The way of Jesus
leads to communion with all people.
His enduring presence in the
Church
is the foundation of a profound
brotherhood
in the world
just as God desires it.

Love the Church as the Lord
Himself.
Though she is burdened with the
weakness
and sinfulness of a long history
she is still the instrument of His
Kingdom,
His work of salvation for the world,
the germ of a new creation.

Rule for a New Brother

**Let us enter more
deeply into the heart
of the Gospel where
the poor have a special
experience of God's
mercy.**

Misericordiae vultus, 15

The Magnificat

My soul glorifies the Lord,
my spirit rejoices in God my
Saviour.
He looks on his servant in her
lowliness;
henceforth all ages will call me
blessed.
The Almighty works marvels
for me.
Holy his name!
His mercy is from age to age,
on those who fear him.
He puts forth his arm in
strength
and scatters the proud-hearted.
He casts the mighty from their
thrones
and raises the lowly.
He fills the starving with good
things,
sends the rich away empty.
He protects his servant Israel,
remembering his mercy,
the mercy promised to our
fathers,
to Abraham and his sons for
ever.

Luke 1:46-55

Mary, Open to God and to the World

Mary opens her hands to God in prayer, but her eyes are open to the world. It is not a bad image for praying. We look without illusion or self-protection at the world, its pain, delight, hunger, grief, hope, and all that informs, shapes our prayer. Praying is not necessarily best described as looking toward God; sometimes, and especially in intercession, it is equally a learning to look at the world as if with God's eyes.

Rowan Williams

Salve Regina
Hail, holy Queen, Mother of Mercy!
Hail, our life, our sweetness, and our hope!
To you do we cry, poor banished children of Eve;
to you do we send up our sighs,
mourning and weeping in this valley of tears.
Turn, then, most gracious advocate,
your eyes of mercy towards us;
and after this our exile, show to us
the blessed fruit of your womb, Jesus.
O clement, O loving, O sweet Virgin Mary.
Pray for us, O holy Mother of God
that we may be made worthy
of the promises of Christ.
Amen.

Hermann of Reichenau
(1013–1054)

Teach My Heart
This Day

O Lord my God,
teach my heart this day
where and how to find you.
You have made me and re-made me,
and you have bestowed on me
all the good things I possess,
and still I do not know you.
I have not yet done
that for which I was made.
Teach me to seek you,
for I cannot seek you
unless you teach me,
or find me.
Let me seek you in my desire;
let me desire you in my seeking.
Let me find you by loving you;
let me love you when I find you.

St Anselm (1033–1109)

The word that came to Jeremiah from the Lord: 'Come, go
down to the potter's house, and there I will let you hear my
words.' So I went down to the potter's house, and there he
was working at the wheel. The vessel he was making of clay
was spoiled in the potter's hand, and he reworked it into
another vessel, as seemed good to him ... Then the word of
the Lord came to me: 'Just like the clay in the potter's hand,
so are you in my hand.'

Jeremiah 18:1-6

Bearers of Peace

Lord, God of peace,
we thank you
for all the longing, all the efforts,
all the striving
that your Spirit of peace
kindles in our time.
Open our spirits and our hearts
still more
to all our brothers and sisters
who are now in need of love,
so that, more and more,
we may become bearers of peace.
Amen.

Blessed Paul VI

Night is Drawing Nigh

**Night is drawing nigh –
For all that has been –
Thanks!
For all that shall be –
Yes!**

Dag Hammarskjøld

… Lord, I have time,
I have plenty of time,
all the time that you give me,
the years of my life,
the days of my years,
the hours of my days,
they are all mine.
Mine to fill, quietly, calmly,
but to fill completely, up to the brim,
to offer them to you, that of their insipid
water
you may make a rich wine
such as you made once in Cana of Galilee.
I am not asking you tonight Lord,
for time to do this and then that,
but your grace to do conscientiously,
in the time that you give me, what you
want me to do.

Michel Quoist

A Heart for Simple Things

Creator God,
give us a heart for simple things:
love and laughter,
bread and wine,
tales and dreams.
Fill our lives
with green and growing hope;
make us people of justice
whose song is Alleluia
and whose name breathes love.

Anon, South Africa

Be Lord Jesus, a bright flame before me,
A guiding star above me,
A smooth path below me,
A kindly shepherd behind me:
Today, tonight and forever.

St Columcille (521–597)

At the end, we will find ourselves face to face with the infinite beauty of God … Even now we are journeying towards the sabbath of eternity, the New Jerusalem, towards our common home in heaven. Jesus says, 'I will make all things new'. (Rv 21:5).

Laudato Si', 243

Entrusting all to the Lordship of Christ

We will entrust the life of the Church, all humanity, and the entire cosmos to the Lordship of Christ, asking him to pour out his mercy upon us like the morning dew, so everyone may work together to build a brighter future.

Misericordiae vultus, 5

The twelve hours of the day (Jn 11:9) are lived fully in the light when they are lived in hope. Hope is not only waiting to attain an arduous, but possible, future good; it is the anticipation of future things promised and given by the Lord who has had time for man, the terrain of his coming where the tomorrow of God comes to take shape in man's present … In hope, today opens onto the horizon of eternity and eternity comes to set up her tents in today.

Carlo Maria Martini

For Christians, all of human life, its joys and hope, its grief and anguish, is lit by the expectation we carry in our hearts as heirs of all that belongs to the Son. Faith heightens the happiness and sorrow, the gifts and losses we experience in life. It never seeks comfort in ignoring or turning away from all that life teaches. Christian faith engages with life, as it is lived day by day, in communion with Jesus Christ, 'the light of humanity', with his Blessed Mother and with all 'who shine with his light and so guide us along our way'.

The Lamp of Love

Grant me, O Lord, the lamp of
love that never grows dim,
that it may shine in me and
warm my heart,
and give light to others through
my love for them,
and by its brightness we may
have a vision of the Holy City
where the true and
inextinguishable light shines,
Jesus Christ our Lord. Amen.

St Columban (d. 615)

Deep peace of the running wave to you,
Deep peace of the flowing air to you,
Deep peace of the quiet earth to you,
Deep peace of the shining stars to you,
Deep peace of the Son of Peace to you.

Celtic blessing

His left hand is beneath my
head, and with his right hand
he embraces me.

Song of Songs 2:6

Acknowledgements

p. 7 Ronald Rolheiser, *Seeking Spirituality*, London: Hodder and Stoughton, 1998, p. 153.

p. 8 Macrina Wiederkehr, 'A Prayer to own your Beauty' from *Seasons of Your Heart: Prayers and Reflections* by Macrina Wiederkehr. Copyright © 1991 by Macrina Wiederkehr. Reprinted by permission of HarperCollins Publishers.

p. 8 Wayne Simsic, *Praying with John of the Cross*, Winona, Minnesota: St Mary's Press, 1993, p. 88. Used with permission.

p. 10 Joseph Duffy, *Patrick in His Own Words*, Dublin: Veritas, 1975, pp. 16–26.

p. 11 *St Patrick's Breastplate,* ascribed to St Patrick, Mrs C. F. Alexander, trans.

p. 15 Henri Nouwen, *The Inner Voice of Love*, London: Darton, Longman & Todd, 2014, pp. 59–60.

p. 26 Timothy Radcliffe, *Seven Last Words*, London: Burns & Oates, 2004, p. 25.

p. 27 *Prayer of St Ignatius*, version by John Foley, *Earthen Vessels*, Missouiri: St Louis Jesuits.

p. 28 Joyce Rupp, 'The Comfort of Others', *Your Sorrow is my Sorrow: Hope and Strength in Times of Suffering*, New York: Crossroad Publishing, 1999, p. 128.

p. 29 Edward J. Farrell, *The Father is Very Fond of Me: Experiences in the Love of God*, Denville, NJ: Dimension Books, 1975, pp. 59–60.

p. 34 Johnny Doherty, *Do You Want To Be Well Again? Thoughts and Prayers at Time of Sickness*, Dublin: Veritas, 2005, pp. 23–24.

p. 36 Christoph Schönborn, *Living the Catechism of the Catholic Church: Volume 2, The Sacraments*, San Francisco: Ignatius Press, 2000, p. 104.

p. 39 Christoph Schönborn, p. 104.

p. 42 Marty Haugen, 'Lamb of God', *Mass of Creation*, 2004. Copyright © 1984 GIA Publications.

p. 43 Brother Roger of Taizé, *Life from Within*, Geoffrey Chapman Mowbray, an imprint of Bloomsbury Publishing Plc., p. 26. Used with permission.

p. 44 John T. Carmody, 'Ecological Consciousness', *The New Dictionary of Catholic Spirituality*, Michael Downey, ed., Collegeville, Minnesota: The Liturgical Press, 1993, p. 332.

p. 44 Catholic Bishops' Conference of Japan, *Reverence for Life: A Message for the Twenty-First Century* (1 January 2000), 89.

p. 47 Michael Downey, *The New Dictionary of Catholic Spirituality*, p. 192.

p. 48 Alan Paton, 'O Lord, Open My Eyes', *Instruments of Peace* Collins/Fontana Books, 2nd ed., 1983.

p. 48 *Rule for a New Brother*, Springfield, IL: Templegate Publishers, 1997, p. 18. Used with permission.

p. 50 Prayer is reproduced with permission from *The Book of Saints*, by Victor Hoagland CP © 2014 by Catholic Book Publishing Corp., NJ. All rights reserved. www.catholicbookpublishing.com

p. 50 Michael Carotta, *Sometimes We Dance, Sometimes We Sing: Embracing the Spiritual Growth of Adolescents*, Orlando, FL: Harcourt Religion Publishers, 2002, p. 77.

p. 51 Donal Neary, *Communion Reflections: For Sundays and Holy Days, Year C*, Dublin: Veritas, 1997, pp. 119–20.

p. 52 *Alive-O 7, Teacher's Book*, Dublin: Veritas, 2003, p. 131.

p. 53 *Rule for a New Brother*, p. 44. Used with permission.

p. 55 Rowan Williams, *Ponder These Things: Praying with Icons of the Virgin*, Norwich: The Canterbury Press, 2002, pp. 52–53.

p. 58 Dag Hammarskjöld, *Markings*, W.H. Auden and Leif Sjöbery, trans., New York: Alfred A. Knopf, 1964, p. 89. Copyright © 1964 by Dag Hammarskjöld. Used by permission of Doubleday, an imprint of the Knopf Doubleday Publishing Group, a division of Penguin Random House LLC. All rights reserved.

p. 58 Michel Quoist, *Prayers*, Lanham MD, Chicago, New York, Oxford: Sheed and Ward, 1963, 1991, 1999, p. 98. Used with permission of Rowman & Littlefield.

p. 60 Carlo Maria Martini, *I Believe in Eternal Life*, London: St Pauls Publishing, 2013, p. 116.

Cover image: Parish Church of Sant Bartomeu & Santa Tecla, Sitges, Catalonia.

All photographs © Gareth Byrne.